BUTTER and LOVE

A Daughter Remembers

Leslie Sandberg

Grosvenor House
Publishing Limited

This book is published by
Grosvenor House Publishing Ltd
Link House
140 The Broadway, Tolworth, Surrey, KT6 7HT.
www.grosvenorhousepublishing.co.uk

A CIP record for this book
is available from the British Library

ISBN 978-1-83975-379-4

DEDICATION

This book is dedicated to my parents,
Shirley Jane Bell Slocumb Sandberg
and
Bernhard Lennart Sandberg,
who brought real love, passion, decency, truth,
joy, and so much more to my life and to the world.

CONTENTS

EPIGRAPH

"I've learned that regardless of your relationship with your parents, you'll miss them when they're gone from your life."

— Maya Angelou

PREFACE

Writing this homage to my parents has given me so many priceless gifts. In short, to know each memory is somehow embedded in my mind after so many years is simply blissful. And, being able to tap into each of them as I have in writing this book or moreover revisiting a diary of my mind seems to have offered a new kind of calm, especially during the times we are now living in due to COVID19. The Virus seemed to invade our everyday lives and moved into our world. Everything was shutting down and that made me sad and reflective. Travel plans ended abruptly along with going to the movies, or theatre, or visiting a gallery. The streets and highways seemed abandoned venues for getting from one place to another. I was stranded or so it seemed and was determined to not become complacent. So, it was a good time to pick up my pen and write. By the way, the year is 2020!

My intention to write happened during an early morning of meditation, exercise, and reflection. And since the regular routines in a pre-COVID19 world only partially remain, I simply felt it was time to share these memories with the world.

Time seemed more abundant, mostly due to the pandemic, and my awareness of that abundance was occurring daily. The daily routine needed adjustment, so I realized the quiet mornings my mother always enjoyed were also important to me and this fueled my willingness to launch this project.

You will see the phrase 'butter and love' mentioned periodically throughout this book. She believed butter and love should be present in everyone's life, be it in the kitchen, or in a daily routine, or in wanting a kind of day to happen. I suppose it was her way of teaching me as a little girl the importance of hope, optimism, and that one could make everything a little bit better if one tried.

I also realized there is never a good or better time to write such a book. In deciding to write it now, I have discovered such a journey has been worth it. I started and stopped so many times over the years. A piece here, a few words there, a quote, or reference to hold onto until I was ready. Well, ready doesn't just appear. It must be invited by self or forced in some way.

I am hopeful it will read more like a memoir, rather than a book. Regardless, I promise this is intended to be a sharing. There is hardly a deep philosophical investigation or even a somewhat scholarly exploration of the relationship I had with my parents. Or what a relationship means in those contexts. Rather, this work is and remains a work of love. If that has come through at all, then it has been worth the effort. This homage is the result of much exploration. At times it hasn't been easy to write, and, accordingly, some of this isn't easy to share. Each word chosen is part of my memory and experiences and how I see this history. It is also from stories told countless times to dear friends and my loving extended family. Every line and especially those with quotations include as much verbatim language as I am able to recall. I know I have missed the mark here and there, although my intentional recall is truly genuine. This has also become a profoundly personal project.

But in choosing each word and what to include, I have come to believe I have learned or remembered some important lessons; new lessons too about the way in which we experience our past, our history. And how each of these experiences become part of our own narrative. I have not treated these memories as a journalist would. Nor was I able to refer to journals and diaries since they no longer exist. You see, they were destroyed in the Tunnel Fire of 1991 (generally referred to as the Berkeley-Oakland Firestorm) when I lost my home, as many others did. Everything was destroyed including the family keepsakes and history.

I also never carried a recorder or iPhone since such technologies haven't always existed to capture ideas, or to jot down fragments of memories.

So, now it must be stated clearly that each word and what is finally written here is mine and mine alone. I did not involve immediate family members although I struggled with that decision. I ultimately concluded this is my story and felt strongly my story needed to be about my memories of our parents and not theirs. That said, I am certain I have not remembered everything perfectly, let alone, fully accurately, but I have tried to be diligent in each recounting. Any and all errors or misunderstandings are my responsibility. Mine alone.

Writing this or anything requires something of a village; writing such a personal statement as this is, requires much more. I am immensely grateful to a small group of people, the most important friendships in my life, one and all. Many have also been colleagues and collaborators over the years, so their reading this is even more meaningful to me. Their willingness to review various drafts and commit the time to do so is also a gift. Although so many ideas offered had value, not all made it onto the page. They helped me see my story more clearly and I hope the final work does honor to each of them, and the thought and effort they put into it. Whatever value may be found on each page, the credit and acknowledgement must go to them. Not only did they encourage me when I doubted myself, all made each page stronger.

I thank you for reading this and trust you will enjoy it. I offer to you, the reader, a collection of memories rather than a chronological history of my parents lives and how they lived, their work ethic, contributions to the community and how they seemed to open up the world for me and so many. Litchfield, Minnesota, our hometown, was a small rural farming community but the smallness didn't matter. Through their efforts, the world I saw was big and open and had no boundaries. A flaw in structuring the book this way may be occasional repetition of information. However, by doing so I felt it would enhance both context and meaning. For that reason, each chapter can stand alone and be read out of order.

I hope you will also see yourself in this effort and reflect on memories you might have of your parents or someone who has been special in your life. My parents inspired me, and while so much of this book is dedicated to who they were and what they did in their lives, and the sacrifices made, I hope I have continued to mirror their beliefs and actions in my life.

ACKNOWLEDGEMENTS

This homage to my parents would not exist without the help, assistance, talent and keen eyes of several people. Their ever-present focus, creativity, and attention to each detail made for a most robust and meaningful collaboration. Countless email exchanges and phone time brought each word to life and helped me to further inform both my memory of my parents and growing up in Minnesota.

Margaret "Peggy" Poggio

What can I say? Peggy is the dearest of dear friends, my best friend, and her talents, while many, also include being a superlative editor. Her exquisite eye for detail always catches the smallest error and, when she brings out her hot pink pen (old style or electronic), watch out! This book has benefitted enormously from her dedication and attention to every detail and her willingness to do so virtually. She enhanced the overall readability, would often question what I meant in a certain passage, and always offered useful advice to further inform the story I was trying to tell. Her unwavering stamina and review of countless drafts was present to the end. Beyond all of this, and for this book, most of the photos used are of her creation. She painstakingly helped me select each image believing it would further inform each page or enhance a memory, be it of travel, theatre, or one yet unknown.

Diana Jahns

Diana is a gifted and talented photographer and designer. She contributed ideas for photos and the cover design. She also brought many photos to life and refreshed or recreated some since so few exist. For this and so much more, I will remain eternally grateful to her and our continuing friendship. Feel free to visit her website at: www.dianajphoto.com.

This book was strengthened with the help of long-time friends who believed in my ability to write this story and offered to read various drafts. I want to acknowledge their contributions. They gave generously of their time to make this book better and, I hope, more interesting to read. A few preferred not to be formally acknowledged. Others gave their permission. They are Barbara Chandler, Gwendolyn Doebbert (a fellow Minnesotan), Richard Epstein, Carol Howle, Jeannine McCune, Poppy Reybin (another Minnesotan), Maurice Smith, and Andrea Verdon.

I

QUIET MORNINGS

Always an early bird, Mum would occupy her mornings with multiple cups of black coffee, reading local and national newspapers, and writing. Next, she would do a deep dive into the stack of books close at hand. There was always an endless pile of books! Whether the sun was peeking through the windows or (as often is the case in Minnesota, our home state) the white of a frigid winter was blinding us with the brightness, there she was, seated at the kitchen table alone. In deference to her space and time and to avoid disturbing her, I would sometimes peek around the corner or, if it was summer, from the downstairs bedrooms.

You see, this was her time — her private time to reflect on life, her kids and family, and the world, be it politics or world affairs. She was well read; she loved history, science, medicine, and most literature. And as we all do, she had a list of favorites. A devoted reader of biographies, she would spend hours on all things Churchill, Lincoln,

Roosevelt and anything written by Steinbeck, Falkner, Twain, Hemingway, Fitzgerald, Lee, Dickinson, Capote, Mitchell, or Miller. I could go on and on but, well, you get the picture. I must note, however, she was not a huge fan of what she would call "pulp." And what is this you ask? Fiction. She wasn't against it per se, but I recall once when I was reading a really good who-done-it novel, she turned to me and asked, "why are you wasting your precious eyesight reading that pulp?" She said nothing else. I didn't respond. Nor did she ask me to stop reading that "pulp"; but in her own way, she would offer up an abundance of "good stuff" to read. She called such an action and many others like it, "non-directive counseling." I did read all that "good stuff," but to this day, I always try to balance it with a good dash of fiction.

As I grew older, I would join her, and she would pour me a cup of coffee (although it would be mostly milk or cream). I always felt grown up. We'd sit and talk about so many things and I would pepper her with questions. She would answer with small stories and memories she kept neatly in her mind but then suggest I visit our book library and read about this or that. You see, there was always an assignment in response to my curiosity. Well darling Leslie, "go look it up as I would have to!" And I did. Without knowing it, she was training me so I could read and learn.

Back at the table each morning, I was ready with more questions. I knew if I asked she would look at me as only a mother can and the glance would speak volumes. Off I'd go to find another book to read.

This routine went on for decades. As I have looked back on those early years with Mum and the years that would follow when we would share a home together, I am ever more grateful for each of them. I appreciate my early mornings even more now because of those memories. Quiet moments are to be treasured. It seems to me now, more than ever, that the quiet invites endurance given the daily rush of life and the hurried pace in which we often find ourselves. And in the currency of the day, endurance is needed more than ever. Thank you, Mum, for all those hours spent together and endless cups of coffee too. And for the discussions that would help me see the value in such a ritual.

Emily Dickinson, a favorite poet of mine, seemed to capture such quintessential nature of mornings in her poem titled 'Will There Really be a Morning' (Dickinson, Emily. *Complete Poems of Emily Dickinson*, Poem 101. 1955). This poem summarizes my quiet mornings with Mum not only because mornings are the start of each new day during which events, small or large, significant, or not, may take place, but a view that every morning is significant.

Will there really be a morning?
By Emily Dickinson

Will there really be a "Morning"?
Is there such a thing as "Day"?
Could I see it from the mountains
If I were as tall as they?

Has it feet like Water lilies?
Has it feathers like a Bird?
Is it brought from famous countries
Of which I have never heard?

Oh some Scholar! Oh some Sailor!
Oh some Wise Men from the skies!
Please to tell a little Pilgrim
Where the place called "Morning" lies!

II

THE KITCHEN

The kitchen, or I should say my mother's kitchen, was always a gathering place for family, friends and drop-ins. It was her place to run and so she did. I have joyful memories of her cooking, baking and preparing meals. She always seemed to make it look so easy and somehow found a way to create food in a decorative fashion; a food architect, if you will. Mum and her mother, our grandmother, Hedwig (although we always called her Nana), and my father's mother, Esther, would join in. Those times must have been very personal and intimate for them. They would plan meals and argue over what to include, or not. You see, dinner time wasn't simply a meal, it was an experience.

Although cookbooks were plentiful, mother usually paid scant attention to what was on the page. She and the grandmothers would modify, create, adjust, and in short, our kitchen became a test kitchen. Old and tattered cookbooks were treated as great treasures. All would have notes and comments in the margins. Everything was modified whether it needed it or not. One old cookbook was kept in a box since the binding was broken, and pages were thin and faded. This treasure was off limits for us kids and only Nana would have power over it.

They would talk or argue endlessly about substituting one ingredient for another and then somehow, agree on who would do what. Nana would always be in charge of pastries and pies. It was not Mum's forte nor did she have any interest in making what she called "that pesky" pie dough. Conversely, Nana had little interest in baking cookies and cakes so naturally Mum would take charge of those creations. Esther confined herself to baking bread. A natural division of labor ensued, and everyone seemed happy to focus on what they enjoyed doing and being able to do together.

Every time I walked into the kitchen, I enjoyed the smell of so many aromas. It filled the room. You could simply close your eyes and be lost in it. Now today if I close my eyes, I can see our kitchen and gaze at the counters and see a big bowl of eggs. Next to the eggs was a bowl of butter from Land O'Lakes (unsalted, of course). Mum always felt cooking or baking should always involve the freshest ingredients and they should be at room temperature.

Evening dinners were filled with conversation and discourse. And we would always watch the CBS Evening News with Walter Cronkite and Eric Sevareid. Later, when 60 Minutes premiered, it too would become a viewing ritual for our family. My mother was particularly excited because 60 Minutes would tell long stories based on in-depth investigation by the 60 Minutes staff. Don Hewitt, brainchild of 60 Minutes, painstakingly selected stories that gave something to every member of any family anywhere. He somehow managed to turn news into a primetime entertainment empire which stands tall even today. Steve Kroft, in a tribute to Mr. Hewitt said, "Don liked to say that 60 Minutes doesn't cover issues — it does stories about people who are swept up in them. It's a technique, he said, as old as time."

So dinner was consumed with conversation about current events, or special occurrences of the day, literature, science, medicine and so on. The discussions were fun, informative, and usually always educational. As kids, this was our norm; we just figured this was what every household experienced nightly. To be well-informed about such things was fundamental to my growing up. And to this day, I relish keeping well-informed of such things, even when the news is dreadful.

As the holidays approached, it seemed as though the entire house was turned into an assembly line. Again, my mother and Nana, along with my father's mother, Esther, would start baking weeks before the holidays since they wanted to be sure the neighbors and others in the community would receive a holiday basket. The baskets were works of art. Personalized for each family or often a widow or widower, they were not only beautiful to look at, but all the goodies were delicious and homemade. Many recipients were literally shut in throughout the cold winters of Minnesota.

Basket goodies included a rich selection of baked goods, homemade deli meats, chocolates and other sweets; and yes, even fruitcake along with selections of brandy or sherry, and the occasional single malt scotch. Every item represented our rich European heritage and culture: Cookies and sweets such as Norwegian butter cookies, Krumkake, Rosettes, Sandbakkels, fig cookies, cranberry walnut cookie balls, petit fours, ginger snaps, fudge, and shortbread; other goodies (usually selected individually for each recipient) such as cheeses, pickled herring, and Grandfather's sausage; and, of course, fruitcake. A special note is needed regarding the choice of fruitcake since I believe it gets a bad rap. It is very misunderstood. Fruitcake is an ancient product, from Egyptian times, when local cooks gathered and brought with them an array of tropical fruits, some of which were preserved by drying in the sun, and they would soon mix them together with honey and some kind of ground meal. Of course, spices were added for taste. I just had to add in a little ancient history here so as to add my voice to others who want fruitcake to garner some much-needed respect. In any event, my Mum always made sure her fruitcake was soaked with brandy or rum and always spared most sweet fruit and cherries. It was nutty, crunchy and barely bound together using bread. Yum!

III

WOMEN OF
INDEPENDENT MEANS

Mum and her mother, our grandmother Nana, were forced to become women of independent means. (Hailey, Elizabeth Forsythe. *A Woman of Independent Means*. Viking, 1978. Chapter title adapted from this book.) It wasn't the turn of the century, a time when women had few choices; but then again, it would be decades before women would be considered equal to men.

Following the premature death of my grandfather, Hugh Slocumb, MD, they worked to ensure the viability of his former medical practice and began to think of ways in which they would have total control over their future. Since the clinic was situated in their large and "stately" home, it seemed to each of them logical to expand the services to in-home residents needing longer-term nursing care. So they set out to convert the big house into a nursing home and offered health care as appropriate, engaging physicians to come by weekly. However monumental this idea must have seemed at the time, they were convinced they both had the energy, skills and will to make it happen. Apparently it didn't take long before the community recognized the importance of their plan to the community. Soon the house welcomed new residents. Their business prospered.

Upon reflection decades later, they would laugh at what they had done almost without thinking. They just said they had little choice and needed to be confident in their abilities. They proved they could be comfortable in their home and also in their finances, while continuing to offer unfailing support and care to the residents for many years. They had become liberated women early on and it would continue to manifest itself in not only who they were, but also in how they regarded their role and position in the community. There were easier pathways for them since close family friends of the day would constantly try to encourage Nana to date and often she would be introduced to potential suitors. You see, as would be said today, 'she was a real catch.' She was a beautiful and elegant woman, well-educated and considered 'of good breeding.' After all, she was the daughter of a respected religious scholar and minister — a so-called pillar of the community. Although Nana would indulge the occasional introduction and honor requests for dinner, she never confessed to anyone she had little interest in any of these potential suitors even if they were "men" of great wealth. I suspect, having discovered her newfound freedom and independence Nana came to appreciate her own domestic heroism. It was not simply social status and financial security, but rather a desire for her own personal and spiritual strength and having the resources acquired in their development.

The lessons learned from those years, primarily out of necessity and tragedy, were shared and passed on to me in any number of ways. Mum would always remind me being a partner to someone, in whatever form it might take, is blissful and love would present itself in many forms throughout a lifetime. She would also counsel me to take care of myself. And to do so in a way that would allow me to become a woman of independent means should circumstances require it.

IV

HOLIDAYS AND CELEBRATING

Celebrating the holidays was a big deal in our home. Mum was always the instigator and would often declare the start of the holidays by saying, "every holiday begins somewhere." As I described earlier, such planning would start in the kitchen, her kitchen. It didn't take long, however, for the whole house to be somehow involved in holiday planning and decorating. She would bring together an annual calendar of sorts, aimed at celebrating formal holidays and seasonal celebrations, such as birthdays or other traditions from around the world. She always felt it was essential to keep our home both traditional and modern so that every corner of the world would be reflected in some way or another.

The most favorite time of the year was, of course, Christmas and leading up to it, Thanksgiving. The house would hint of holly, evergreen, and mistletoe, and each room would be adorned and decorated accordingly. Candles would be ever present and lit daily, a tradition I continue to this day. For decades, we would enjoy a living tree, decorated in splendor beginning mid-November and would be lovingly cared for well into the new year. The season was long as I look back, but it never felt that way. Occasionally, Mum would ask Dad to help flock a tree, and he would patiently work with her as she selected the color for the season, be it white, hints of red, pink, or even an off-color blue. She would coordinate gift wrapping to compliment the theme for the year. We didn't have a flocked tree every year, but when we did, it was spectacular.

Our home was Christmas Central. Mum and Dad would host holiday dinners and parties because of our elegant dining room and of course, the food! I have vivid memories of watching people's faces as they would enter the formal dining room, smile and gasp. You see, it wasn't just the smells and various aromas filling every space, the tree would be twinkling in the corner and a wreath would welcome each guest, along with music in the background. It was truly the 'season to be jolly.'

The large mahogany dining table would welcome each table setting, adorned with Royal Doulton or Spode china, Grande Baroque sterling tableware, and vintage, etched Fostoria glassware. Handwritten place cards, candles, festive decorations and a centerpiece would grace the table and complete the scene, unforgettable to all.

These memories remain vivid in my mind since I would usually set the table (with some direction from Mum) although she would simply tell me to make it beautiful. She would review my work and make modest adjustments, here and there, mostly to check that each setting complied with her standards. What standards you might ask? This refers to the ideal amount of space from the center of one place setting to the center of the next place setting, allowing each guest plenty of elbow room.

Historically, and in what would be referred to as "fine houses," the butler would use his butler's stick to take such measurements. Similarly, Mum would also measure the back of each chair to the edge of the table to ensure it was 24". Again, this would allow guests to sit comfortably. You see, it was her belief that the food served would simply taste better if the scene was equally "delicious." To this day, I try in my own way to honor some of her traditions, although the currency of modern times allows for less formality. Nonetheless, I still set a fine table.

The food and feasting would continue for days and days, and friends and others would stop by knowing there was always some good treat at our house, or scrumptious leftovers, and of course, coffee, tea, brandy, or sherry. For example, sandwiches with cranberry sauce were a reward for the hard work needed to prepare various holiday dinners. And, using all the best tidbits for soup stock, including the turkey carcass, would guarantee something new and wonderful in winter. The music of the holidays would play softly in the background well into the wee hours of the morning. So many memories. I still decorate to this day and smile in doing so. Why not? After all, it is the most wonderful time of the year.

V

POLITICS AND OTHER MUSINGS

Politics (within the context of history) always mattered deeply to my parents. Their devotion to reading encompassed a mixture of critical reviews of our nation's past and present, and the political cultures and environment in which lessons could be learned, and hopefully the worst of them not repeated. It was also a topic they felt where reading offered a rare gift, an opportunity to look back. Not that such reading would offer high-minded advice even if based on hard fought wars, blood, tears, and sacrifice. Such immersion by each of them would always include the latest in science and medicine, new discoveries, and anything else that might just make the world a better place for us all.

They bequeathed the same devotion upon me; a desire and hunger to remain a student and critic of history and politics. They only asked and reminded me to try to challenge myself, my thinking and ideas, and to form my own opinions. Most of all, they wanted me to remain humble enough to admit when any opinion or belief needed revision. They always challenged me to think about my opinions in light of a changed time in our history. In short, not to be stuck on a single-minded belief or attitude since seasons change, as do the times, and they require us to review the past and ensure the future is better. Finally, we all should try to make the future better in any way we could.

Mum went further in her political world than did Dad. She was more vocal and would, by any definition today, be considered an activist. She had always held strong beliefs about equality between men and women, and this she would strongly instill in me. For her, the belief or idea that it was a woman's obligation or destiny to only marry and bear children was foreign to her. I am not sure to this day that she thought she would ever marry, let alone have children. She did, however, believe strongly that people were equal and would spend much of her life devoted to reading countless newspapers, watching the news, and glued to the television anytime there was a pending election. I would find her sitting at the kitchen table making notes and calculating who would win. It did not matter that she would be sleep starved. She wanted to know the results as they came in.

Her activism was innate; something that was as natural to her as breathing. Unlike so many of her contemporaries that had similar interests, her interest in politics did not arise because of her war service. Those that would start to engage in politics and "carry the flag" would often do so because of their experiences during World War II (WWII). Most were homemakers prior to the war, and those that worked outside the home usually worked in jobs as secretaries, receptionists, or department store clerks. Once America entered the war, and men went off to war by the millions, it was then that women stepped into either civilian or military jobs that were left vacant. They were proud to serve their country but many felt this was a temporary gap to be filled. My mother never felt this way. She had always worked and she and her mother, Nana, were already "women of independent means" so the notion of a newfound interest in fighting for social change and equality was not new at all. It was already there. They neither needed WWII posters nor did they need images of confident-looking women to flex their political muscles. They were already their own "Rosie the Riveter." And they were already very self-sufficient.

Despite the call for women to work, it was only intended to be temporary and women were fully expected to leave their jobs and return to their domestic lives as the men returned from war. Well, it did not turn out that way. Some were okay with this notion but many others wanted to continue their work or they were intent on finding other work, now filled with confidence and skills. Men could no longer claim any level of superiority over women. Women had enjoyed a kind of freedom like never before, and many thrived on knowing that they could have both financial and personal independence. Many wanted more.

In Mum's case, her commitment to important ideals was simply an ongoing extension of her already complex life. She always dedicated time to write letters to politicians on both sides of the aisle and argue rigorously for their commitment to one issue or another. And if there was no response from them, she would pick up the phone and dial their number. I heard her often say, "This is Shirley Sandberg. We have a problem and you are going to help me with it." She was polite but always direct. It was rare that the office of so-and-so elected official did not take note and it was even more rare for her not to receive a callback. She was intent in her pursuit. I asked her once why she did not give up, knowing that she might not get anywhere. She answered directly and specifically, and quoted one of her heroes, Harry Truman. She said, "I believe as Mr. Truman did. It's one thing to work hard and to stay the course when you think you're going to win, but it's quite another thing when you know you're going to lose."

Mum would tell me many stories about her letter writing, phone calls with politicians and important political events she witnessed in her early life. One was the presidential election of 1948. Heading into Election Day, November 2, 1948, it was a foregone conclusion that Thomas Dewey had the Presidency in the bag. Numerous polls, politicians, reports, and pundits predicted an easy win over Harry Truman. However, the surprise victory of Harry Truman in the early hours of November 3 would become part of our country's political lore and a great American story. Mum knew that Truman would win since she believed that underdogs always have a chance. And Truman was certainly the underdog. She proudly would say that it was one of the greatest moments she would ever see in American politics.

Another seminal moment was Watergate and the Watergate Hearings. From the moment this political scandal was made public, and news centers reported the break-in of the Democratic National Headquarters, Mum was again glued to the set. So was I. The hearings were broadcast "gavel-to-gavel" nationally by PBS and aroused wide public interest. It easily became an all-consuming event for many Americans. People would take sick days or rush home to watch the hearings, and daily conversations at work would turn away from other events of the day to only what was happening in Washington, D.C. My mother knew it would eventually be Nixon's downfall. What she did not predict is it would take over two years until he would resign, following re-election in 1972.

It was a complete and utter fall from grace. Following so close on the tragedy of the Vietnam War, here again the country was witnessing such secret corruption and asking disturbing questions about government and our values. Although the political bloodletting was thought to help heal a nation, sadly, suspicion and doubt lingered and rebuilding faith in democracy would remain a fragile journey for many.

It did not take a national scandal for my parents to act on their fervent belief in decency and equality. They also stood up for people who were oppressed and did not like bullies nor tolerate those who would not accept people from diverse backgrounds. I knew this was a lifelong belief but certainly was cemented given their service during WWII. It was, after all, so much about oppression. They had simply seen too much of this in their lifetimes and throughout so many experiences during WWII. My mum would not like the lack of a coherent conversation and discourse present today. I think that is why we had straight talk and deep discussions over dinner while watching the evening news. We were not asked to agree with what was being said but we were invited to comment and offer opinions even though we were young. It shaped me. It shaped all of us.

In looking back now to all those dinners and arguments, I appreciate more than ever the lens they gave me. Throughout their lives, they continued to hope future generations would not have to fight world wars, and America would seek to find better angels and become a more perfect democracy.

I guess we are all still working on that goal.

VI

FAITH, SPIRITUALITY, AND DOUBT

Where do I begin? In writing this, it dawned on me to not include a chapter on faith, spirituality, and doubt would dishonor my parents. Each had a very personal view of such. All throughout my early or what one might call formative years, Mum and Dad shared their observations on centuries long running arguments between believers and non-believers. It was always informative, usually humorous, occasionally irreverent, but we would discuss such things often. It was clear their lives and experiences helped inform an ever-changing view of faith, spirituality, and doubt.

Mum always struggled with this since she was so grounded in knowing belief lies within the good and bad of human history. She was also grounded in medicine and science. It is not that she was a nonbeliever but rather, she questioned and had doubts. I recall us watching the seminal series "Faith and Reason" which featured a collection of conversations focused on this subject and the space between them. The series was in the tradition of the previous landmark series, "Power of Myth" that featured Joseph Campbell, famed mythologist, and was hosted by Bill Moyers, lauded American journalist and political commentator. It was during this series Mum arrived at what would become her mantra for years to come. Essentially, she was neither wholly a believer nor wholly a skeptic and she would always include science as a way to illuminate her beliefs.

My dad, on the other hand, held his understanding of faith or spirituality quietly. He didn't speak of it often but demonstrated his beliefs in his approach to most everything and everyone. People from the community seemed to sense he was the kind of person they could talk to, or confide in. His smile was easy and when they were in his presence, I could tell they wanted to pour out their worries and darkest secrets. I know this happened often although he would never share anything nor would I ask. It simply wasn't done and I knew that. I do know that somehow they left transformed. And somehow, perhaps felt better about their own struggles.

After his death, I learned quickly about his empathy and how he touched so many people throughout his life. They would tell Mum and all of us that they had never met anyone like him and some spoke emotionally of Dad's compassion and humility. A few would also say that at times, he could be frank and direct. It seemed that his life experience, especially during his service, would be brought to bear on such private conversations. In short, it was not a private discussion based on sentimentality. Rather, every word seemed to come from his experiences shared without judgement.

Dad rarely voiced any doubts or worries about the business or anything else. And if he had them, he certainly kept them to himself. Generally, and especially when Mum was worried, he would always reach out and touch her arm and simply say, "everything is going to be ok." I always felt that, while remaining grounded in science, his steadfast belief system seemed to resonate fully in him and no doubt came from confronting the horrors of war as he was forced to do.

Overall, the doubts they both had and any doubts I or any of us have are not necessarily a bad thing. I believe they can help guide us through our own life journey and help us to find inner peace in the long run. I believe this is how they came to an acceptance of their respective "faith" and would continually pass along lessons for me and my siblings to learn in our own way.

VII

LOVE OF THEATRE, MUSIC, ART, AND BOOKS

I have always loved books, music, art, and all things theatrical. Anyone who knows me even a little knows this. I could jokingly blame my parents for my love and addiction to the arts, but in all fairness, I grew up in a household watching films of all kinds, from Judy Garland and Gene Kelly, to John Wayne and Jimmy Stewart. Watching old movies as I did, it was equally hard to escape other interests such as singing, piano lessons, or a drive to Minneapolis to see a film at the Cinerama or live theatre at the Guthrie. My parents always made time for such things.

They invested in theatre recordings of the great works of Shakespeare or other plays. I recall playing the vinyl LP stereo records over and over again. They were always in a boxed set, produced by The Shakespeare Recording Society, Caedmon Records, and would feature any number of famed artists — Paul Scofield (an English actor of stage and screen) or those less well known. I would sit and listen for hours to these voice recordings while reading the actual text. Or by contrast, I would listen to a recording of *The Glass Menagerie*, by Tennessee Williams, one of the greatest playwrights of the 20th century.

Our formal living room also housed an extensive book collection and seemed to be more of a library than a living room. I could easily lose myself for hours reading and did so especially during the polar and frigid Minnesota winters. I continue to feed my addiction of live theatre and am lucky to enjoy such diversity in performances. Live performances, I believe, are the best form of storytelling because they unite all art forms and combine the language of the concrete world with the abstract, the mystical, and often the wonder of music and dance. These become collaborators to help us embrace our thoughts, emotions, and deepest beliefs.

Beyond the simple pleasure of such an experience, live performances promote connections among people and can profoundly improve our understanding of ourselves, and of humanity in a larger, more global sense.

Over so many years I thought about the investment my parents made in books and records, and theatre for our benefit, along with their own enjoyment. It has been important in helping me appreciate a bigger world, acknowledge other cultures and peoples, and to know such engagement brings us together.

VIII

SERVICE TO COUNTRY

My parents served in World War II. They were among the millions who served and sacrificed, demonstrating the kind of courage and honor that resonates to this day. They served not for fame, recognition, or fortune but only because it was the right thing to do. Their service was so powerfully detailed in the best-selling book by Tom Brokaw, *The Greatest Generation.* "It is a generation that, by and large, made no demands of homage from those who followed and prospered economically, politically, and culturally because of its sacrifices. It is a generation of towering achievements and modest demeanor; a legacy of their formative years when they were participants in and witness to sacrifices of the highest order." I mention the above book specifically since it is the kind of book my mother would have read without interruption and would have expected us all to read.

Shirley J. Sandberg (US Army, Nursing)

My mother often spoke of her service. She did so willingly because her first love was nursing and caring for others. Naturally these stories would spill out of her. She was stationed at Camp Atterbury, Indiana. She would become emotional when she would reminisce about "those days" and would tell me about the men she helped through difficult surgeries and other injuries, emotional and psychological. She would come to know them well. They would come to know her, too. It didn't take long before these soldiers would just call her "Ma." They were "her boys" after all and she was devoted to their care and healing. Although they were young when they went to war, filled with grit, passion, strength, and so on, they returned older, broken and battered physically and psychologically.

Calling Mum "Ma" was a term of endearment, but moreover, each young man soon learned she was a force of nature and not one to question how to behave relative to their injuries. She insisted they fight hard to recover.

She helped them heal in all ways one can help someone. She also committed countless hours in helping to build a first-rate psychiatric and burn ward. Such a ward to address injuries of the mind would today be called a clinic for Post-Traumatic

Stress Disorder (PTSD). It wasn't labeled that way during WWII, or earlier wars. Though it was referred to by other names — shell shock, combat fatigue, neuropsychiatric disorders — the emotional toll would extend to the immediate postwar years, and military psychiatric hospitals across the nation were full of afflicted soldiers. Although the term shell shock is rarely used today, it was common throughout World War I (WWI) and WWII.

The term was originally named by Charles Samuel Myers, a British psychologist who used it to describe a type of post-traumatic stress disorder many soldiers were afflicted with during and after the war. This, of course, was long before it was renamed PTSD. The concept of shell shock was ill-defined and could be interpreted as either a physical or psychological injury, or tragically, a lack of moral fiber. Sadly, willful cultural amnesia would settle in, inspired by the stigma of mental health issues and the prevailing male ethos of the strong, silent type. By the 1990's, there remained a reluctance to face reality about the psychological costs of warfare and the punishing consequences. Those costs, as hard as a nation tried to ignore them, did not go away. Soldiers interviewed over a two-decade period, and tens of thousands like them, suffered painful memories. They and their families were left to suffer in silence and isolation.

Mother spent countless hours listening to her boys, writing letters back home, or reading letters out loud to them. Occasionally, she would have to read a letter to them about a loss of life at home or a letter from a girlfriend ending the relationship. Commonly referred to as "Dear John" letters, each soldier would need to learn his beloved wasn't able to cope with certain injuries, be they psychological or physical. The fact a soldier no longer had two arms, legs or was permanently burned and scarred was often "too much" for a girlfriend to manage. These were always the most heartbreaking letters for Mum to read aloud. Ultimately, there would be a long silence and then she would simply tell them they deserved better and "so-and-so" didn't deserve them. She would go on to tell them there would be a special someone back home to love and give love; and not to give up, ever. She insisted they stay in touch with her and many did.

She always believed this level of nursing was far more central to a soldier's recovery than simply treating the physical injuries a soldier suffered. Knowing you can generally repair a physical wound represented an expected challenge, but repairing a wound of the heart, mind, or soul — well, that was even more challenging. I remember vividly her sharing detailed medical photos of pre- and post-surgery wound care, especially burn wounds. It was heart-breaking. Each photo had specific meaning and a story to be told and then, the page would turn, and I would see new photos and the area photographed would show signs of improvement. You could see new skin emerging and healthier color from the extensive skin grafts. Proud of her efforts, she and her boss, Col. Blocker (a military surgeon and chief of plastic surgery and later chief of surgery at the Wakeman General Hospital situated in Camp Atterbury) worked even longer hours to improve wound management and associated infection control since the medical quarters were small, increasing the infection risk. Although a day turned into night into dawn, Mum would write letters to ask (or beg) for additional medical supplies. Rarely did a day pass in which she did not send yet another letter requesting supplies. Frustrated over the lack of supplies, she finally called her mother, our Nana, and asked if she would pack up their home-based medical office, and ship everything she could to her directly at Camp Atterbury. Nana didn't hesitate and did so, wrapping each instrument and repackaging supplies to ensure their safe travel. This way, at least Mum was sure she would have state-of-the-art medical instruments and supplies till the war office could send more.

Mum's experience as a nurse stateside was something she would never forget, and as I have described above, she would recount those days throughout her life. However, there was a time early in her army career when she was asked to serve in the European theatre, specifically England, and help establish tent hospitals and prepare for the expected influx of casualties. She eagerly said yes. Her interest in doing so was based on duty to country and service, but she also wanted to serve overseas. Most of her ancestors and heritage were English so naturally she yearned to spend time there, regardless of the circumstances. Her mother, our Nana, wasn't too keen on the idea but respected her wishes and ultimately gave her unconditional support.

Mum and other nurses were briefed on their assignment and what they could expect. They were also informed about the challenges and danger, and potentially difficult conditions under which all would live and work. These conditions would be ongoing as they treated others and, as a consequence, they could also suffer from various tropical illnesses and diseases since they would need to adapt quickly to different environmental conditions. None of this dissuaded her or others, nor did it diminish their eagerness or commitment in going. And even when the nursing core was informed they had to cope with inadequate supplies and lack of appropriately adapted "theatre" clothing, and there would also be risk in being taken prisoner, they again remained committed to their decision.

About the time she was to embark on this journey, she was informed her orders had been changed. Actually they had been cancelled. In short, she was told she would remain stateside in her current role. Shocked and angered, Mum was determined to find out why and more importantly, who made this decision. She soon discovered it was her boss, Dr. Blocker. She rushed to his office and demanded an explanation, foregoing any normal chain of command. He simply said she was too valuable to him at this time. Period. He further stated she should feel complimented, but Mum would have none of that and told him so. Regardless, it was too late to reissue the orders and she begrudgingly accepted the decision.

Dr. Blocker got the silent treatment for days and weeks but gradually she softened to her fate and forgave him. Well, not completely, but sufficiently so they could again resume the deep and abiding professional partnership they had always enjoyed. I am not sure she ever forgave him completely.

However, something else did make the trip, her personal trunk. Although efforts were made to retrieve the trunk filled with Mum's personal clothes, books, and other items, it seemed to just disappear, just be gone. Ironically, it finally arrived one day, patched together with tape and rope, battered and punished for the long journey it had taken. Mum opened the trunk only to find all her belongings were ruined. No surprise. There was little trace as to where it had been or how many miles it had traveled. Efforts were made to find out, mostly out of curiosity, but all failed. Wherever it had been simply remained a mystery.

Bernhard L. Sandberg (Captain, US Army Air Corps)

My father spent his war years stationed at Hickam Air Force Base, Honolulu, Hawaii, the principal army airfield in Hawaii. Hickam was the focal point with defense planning for the Pacific and aircraft were brought to Hawaii throughout 1941 in preparation for potential hostilities. By December of 1941, the base had become an integrated command for slightly more than one year and consisted of 754 officers and 6,706 enlisted men, with 233 aircraft assigned at three primary bases: Hickam, Wheeler Field, which is now called Wheeler Army Airfield, and Bellows Field, now called Bellows Air Force Station. Hickam was the only one large enough to manage the big bombers such as the B-17 Flying Fortress bomber or the B-24 Liberator, an American heavy bomber. My father served as the chief navigator on the B-24 Liberator and, with his fellow crewmates, completed over 38 missions.

I should state now he didn't speak of these years often, unless we were watching old WWII war movies. I rarely missed times when we could watch such films together. I always hoped he would share more stories and memories or answer my endless questions. Occasionally he would accommodate this curious child. And I listened and learned and remembered. He would tell me about the importance of the B-17 and B-24 and why the B-24 was used extensively in WWII. You see, it served every branch of the American armed forces and several Allied air forces and navies because it was considered a long-range plane. Along with the B-17, they seemed to be the real mainstays of the US strategic bombing campaign throughout the Pacific, including the bombing of Japan, and in the Western European theatre.

Having never before lived anywhere other than his hometown of Litchfield, Minnesota, I can only imagine what he was thinking and how he was feeling to suddenly be stationed in Hawaii and to find himself embroiled in one mission after another. You see, my dad was highly decorated although we didn't know of his bravery and honors until after his death. Even Mum didn't know anything as he hadn't shared it with her. So literally, I grew up not knowing the full extent of my father's achievements, and for the most part, it stayed that way. I recall my father saying only this, "we did what we had to do, and it needs to stay that way." Generations have passed and this attitude remains true for so many WWII veterans. Most have taken their experiences and stories to their graves now.

What is even more astonishing is my father, a highly honored and decorated soldier, considered himself a pacifist. He did not believe in warfare and violence of any kind. However, his belief did not extend to self-defense or in the protection of others. As knowledge of Hitler became known and with the entry of the United States into the war following the bombing of Pearl Harbor, his choice was obvious, serve. He said it was simply, "clarity of purpose": to stop Hitler and the Holocaust and to fight to end the war. Regardless, the issue would cut him deeply and his emotions for years to come would remain in disarray on the question of war. I do not feel he ever found reconciliation in his thoughts and seemed to suffer alone in silence. It is not that he misunderstood the political realism of the time or the degree of intensity with which the effects of war linger. What is left now for my father and mother and their legacy is similar to that of the millions who served and the many heroic and selfless deeds which are etched in history, unknown to millions more. Those few veterans still alive would simply say they served.

IX

THE POST WAR YEARS
"HUNGRY YEARS"

When WWII finally ended in the summer of 1945, life seemed to gradually return to normal. Those who served, including my parents, returned home and would find peacetime jobs or contemplate what to do next. My parents married toward the end of the war having met unexpectedly during home leave; happenstance, as Mum called it, or perhaps serendipity. Neither ever thought they would marry but it happened. They then decided to escape and find peace and hopefully solitude. They settled in the area of International Falls, near Fort Crossing, which connected the cities of International Falls, Minnesota, and Fort Frances, Ontario, Canada. Called "at the place of the inlets," this remote area had been known to explorers, missionaries, and voyagers as early as the 17th century. It had been inhabited by many indigenous peoples and was still very remote in large part because of the frigid weather and eventually promoted itself as the "Icebox of the Nation." My parents didn't mind the cold and the locals felt the overall colder months would help keep this area protected from outside influences; in short, keeping it remote. They liked it that way.

They lived very quietly in a modest two-room log cabin with a wood-burning stove, and the bare necessities. It seemed their lives could now hold something they hadn't experienced for years: stability, silence, and humility. Unable to experience any of these during their service, I have to believe they desperately needed this sanctuary both in terms of the quiet community available to them but also to seek peace in their daily routine. There was no real plumbing to speak of and Dad would chuckle years later as he told me he "fixed up" a water supply to shower, cook, and so on. They settled into their new quiet life and would always refer to those years as the "hungry years." I know these years were probably some of the happiest years for them both.

They had an Irish Setter named Teddy (Mum was always naming dogs after key figures in history and others she admired) and Dad spent hours in the wilderness and forest. He then went to work for the Weyerhaeuser Lumber Company. I must note here my memory is sketchy since this time of their life together wasn't discussed often. Yet, Dad loved nature and would mention his work with the Weyerhaeuser Lumber Company often. He seemed to be naturally skilled in knowing how to manage a forest and timber harvesting operation and to help protect old growth coupled with the regeneration of seedlings for the future. He told the firm he would only work for them if this was equally important to them. They agreed.

Mum settled into her work and offered her skills as a nurse, teaching various techniques to the local community. Since there were no health care services for miles, she felt it was important to educate the local community so they could help each other. She also had a secondary motive which was to help the young people seek more formalized training and see some of the world outside their small community. It worked and for years, Mum would receive mail from many of them sharing their stories. Some left and didn't return and others returned and established businesses of their own.

Life was simple and offered what they both needed, a place where they could find relief from the war. As I reflect on what was shared by them, and realizing they intentionally chose a remote area, away from everything and everyone, it is more evident now they needed this quiet and the psychological escape from memories and trauma of WWII. Although each had very different experiences, they both witnessed the horrors and outcomes of warfare. It was a kind of psychological "load shedding." For the most part, they self-healed and found ways to work through difficult memories or developed defenses that would stay with them throughout their lives. They, like so many others of their generation, didn't seek mental health services. And if one wanted to do so, resources were not only scarce, the cultural stigma associated with it was severe, not unlike it is today. In short, it was felt they just needed to "get over it" and move on. Most tried to do just that and literally suffered in silence.

Sadly, the decades that followed would mark a return to traumatic memories and any defenses used previously simply didn't work as well. I suspect it was true for my parents and recall their leaving us with our grandmother, Nana, so they could escape somewhere. Usually they were gone for an afternoon but sometimes, they would be away for several days. I never asked where they had been or why they went away. Nor did they volunteer such information. And I sensed I should not ask. After all, it really wasn't my business.

I guessed then, and still do, that they simply needed to have the kind of quiet and escape they enjoyed shortly after their service. I believe it was their way of managing their mental health.

Life became a bit more complicated when two children were born, a boy and girl, fraternal twins; my brother and sister. It was 1950 and life would never be the same. Mum knew she was expecting but didn't know there were to be two. She was only able to see a doctor once and he indicated there was only one. What no one knew is the heartbeats were synchronized so what seemed like one baby was really two. It was a surprise for the family and most especially for Dad. As Mum and Dad would learn later, the local community seemed to know Mum was having twins since this area is blessed with communities of several native American tribes. The local tribal leaders who were well known to my parents apparently seemed to sense this, and while there is no real way of knowing why this was so, both Mum and Dad accepted their wisdom to be part of their rich cultural tradition deeply bathed in spirituality.

Shortly after the twins arrived, the townspeople gathered at Mum and Dad's log cabin and gave them 144 handmade and embroidered diapers. The community accepted and welcomed them.

It wasn't long before Mum and Dad would relocate back to Litchfield, Minnesota, Dad's hometown. Mum wasn't keen on the idea but knew it was important to him, so she supported the decision. This decision would lead to opening their own business, focused on engineering, tooling and design. Again, life would be forever changed.

Nana would be their angel investor and funded the business in total. Nana committed $20,000 to the enterprise. Although it seems like a rather modest amount of money today, the purchasing power back then would be just shy of $215,000 in today's money. Nana would eventually move to Litchfield and join the family. She would remain with us the rest of her life and be central in ours.

Dad's parents lived next door. I came along in 1955. As a child, one doesn't think too much of having grandparents so close by, but as I look back on all those years, it was a blessing. Suffice to say they all loved their grandchildren, and the relationships were magical. Enjoying such a multi-generational family is certainly less common now but when I was little, it was simply familiar. Although family dynamics would present some challenges, mostly for Mum, I also know my interest in and affinity for working with older people resulted from these early years. I was always comfortable with older people and seemed to meld into their conversations more easily than I could with friends my age. The times I spent with my grandparents were precious and I learned so much about their generation, the joys and struggles they faced, and how each of them wanted an easier life for their descendants.

X

A REFLECTION, SMALL TOWN LIVING

Litchfield, Minnesota, a small prairie town, is not unlike the mythical town of Lake Wobegon, made famous in Garrison Keillor's "A Prairie Home Companion." There are many such towns scattered throughout the United States and the world. Shaped by their original Native American residents followed by European exploration and settlement, these communities would eventually emerge around various industries such as fur trading, logging, farming, and later, through railroads and iron mining.

What remains common is many people leave these small communities and do not return. However, what is also common is even those who moved permanently always remember their birthplace and how those early years shaped their beliefs and attitude toward others and life in general. In some manner, this allows each of us to go home again, at least in our minds and memories.

That is how it works for me, even today. Growing up in a small town added to the overall influence my parents had on me. It made me a dreamer and encouraged my ambition. And it kept me grounded. We'd make frequent trips to Minneapolis, literally 68 miles due east from Litchfield, and take long drives on the weekend, usually Sundays, to simply explore the countryside. I suspect my love of travel started then and it launched an imagination into what would become my world experience.

Everyone knew our names and a sense of community was ever-present. Conversely some downsides presented themselves. For example, my parents nearly always conducted their business outside the city limits. This would include banking, grocery shopping, etc. Even the engineering business was situated just outside city limits. This was Mum's doing. You see, gossip of any kind always seemed to travel at light speed, especially in a small town. Whether true or not, it didn't matter. Mum would often say, "it's nobody's business what we do."

I think she longed to be more invisible and have what often larger cities offer, anonymity. She had enjoyed such privacy growing up and hoped we would at least be able to experience it one day. Furthermore, she would tell me I needed to see more of the world, experience its diversity of cultures and people, and learn to understand and appreciate people of all walks of life. She was right, of course, since Litchfield could not have afforded this since it was much too small.

My memories of Litchfield are mostly positive and they are grounded in the knowledge my parents were admired and respected throughout the community. I learned this decades later when I visited the area and also when I was invited to present work on technology and telemedicine in Minneapolis, Minnesota, to a healthcare and medical center. I recall being introduced and thanking everyone for the warm invitation to visit them and discuss the growing trends of technology and healthcare. I barely moved away from the introduction when a voice from the back of the auditorium yelled out, "Are you Shirley and Bernie's daughter? Did you know Dr. and Mrs. Slocumb?" Well, as you can imagine, the rhythm of what I hoped would be a well-rehearsed presentation collapsed. I had to respond and simply said, "yes." Thinking this would satisfy whoever it was, I tried again to regain my composure and begin again. It didn't work. The voice asked for more details and this time, I replied, "Might you stand up and introduce yourself so we all know who you are. And ladies and gentlemen, if you don't mind indulging this for a moment . . ." Well, as is the custom in

Minnesota, people are "Minnesota nice." Most chuckled and fell silent. The older gentleman stood up and we discussed where I was from, etc. It seemed to satisfy him and I promised him we would talk more after the presentation. Everyone applauded and I went on to complete the presentation, answer questions, and so on.

The point here is simple. This older gentleman knew who I was because I was the daughter of Shirley and Bernie Sandberg. And he knew who my Mum's parents were because his parents knew them. So, I will remain forever grateful for growing up in a small town and rural community.

XI

GRAND CENTRAL STATION

The chapter title is from my Mum. It seemed as though our home was a gathering place for all things fun. Games, outside sports such as volleyball, badminton, football, or softball. It didn't matter. We were fortunate to have a clear acre of good turf independent of our house. Adjacent to it of course, it offered the perfect locale for such activities. Friends would gather and play their hearts out and somehow, they also knew they would be fed and nourished with a home cooked meal, fresh iced tea or lemonade, and any number of choices for dessert. This would go on all summer. How my parents tolerated the noise and activity, I wonder to this day. So many kids.

Often some of the athletes, a.k.a. friends, would eventually spend the night so sleepovers were common. We would literally occupy the basement of our home and turn our attention to endless games such as Monopoly or Scrabble. Again, food would be provided, with love, and soon Mum would confirm whether everyone wanted to stay over or needed a lift home. It was an easy question to answer and soon my parents would call other parents asking if it would be ok for a stay-over, promising to return all non-Sandberg children to their rightful home in the morning. I don't recall anyone ever saying no. Once all parental permissions were granted and the verdict rendered, bedlam began. It was ok. All in good fun and safe in the knowledge everyone was ok to stay up until the wee hours of the morning and, as long as some simple house rules were honored, hey, have fun.

Of course more food appeared. More games, chatter, and laughter until everyone collapsed into a deep sleep. There was no need for an alarm clock since the morning aroma of fresh baked bread, bacon and other breakfast goodies worked it's magic.

Mum would quickly summon us all, requesting our presence post showers, and so on. Somehow she had a gift of acting like a staff sergeant in the marines without it seeming so.   I think this 'gift' of hers may have been honed during her time as a nurse in the military which required her to be efficient, organized, and firm with patients tempered with a genuine warmth, compassion, and humanity to those in her charge. Everyone would again gather at the kitchen table and soon cars would arrive to collect non-Sandberg kids. For those that needed a ride, my good father would serve as taxi driver.

The feel-good factor was priceless. As I think of those days, I doubt I realized at the time the enormous gift they would again give to me, and my friends. I don't believe I thanked them enough. I am sorry about that.

I still love small gatherings with friends, be it one-on-one, or with a few beloved friends. I don't pretend to be the kind of cook or chef my Mum or Nana was, but there are several key dishes I am known for and I set a beautiful table. And I love very good wine. So when I still endeavor to make it memorable for that special someone, I hope they will find pure pleasure in it. I know I do.

XII

THE SHOP, A LIFETIME OF ENGINEERING

My father was the son of a blacksmith. However, Grandfather was more than that; he was also an inventor. As such, it was only natural Dad would become interested in working with his hands and become enthralled with engineering. Why? Well, he loved fixing things, solving problems, and figuring out why things work the way they do. Or, was it possible to make them work better? Regardless, Mum always believed this suited his personality, quiet ways, and reflective nature.

I can recall seeing him sitting at the kitchen table, reading journals and focused on his own designs. He was always designing or redesigning one thing or another and would capture questions that would stump him. At least for the moment. This would go on for hours, and usually well into the night. It was quiet then and he could remain lost in his thoughts easily and without interruption.

Mum would be there, too, but she would be immersed in a good book.

Being born and raised in a small rural town, and a town noted for farming, Dad's skills in fixing things were in constant demand. Farming equipment always needed repair and often required replacement parts. And even with the advent of John Deere, waiting for parts to arrive in a small town, without the likes of Amazon, UPS, or FedEx, could devastate a farmer's business quickly. As a consequence, the local motto soon became "call Bernie." Dad would stop other business, or simply stay and work later in the evening and re-design the part, build it from scratch, and install the part the following morning. And when the replacement part did arrive, it served as a back-up. It didn't take long for people to realize Dad's design and build was far superior to normal replacement parts. He did his own tooling you see and was gifted in simply making things better.

Other local businesses would call upon him often and the one I remember vividly was the local woolen mill. It employed many people, so when equipment failed, the consequences could really devastating. No work, no pay. My dad always did work for the owner and as usual in business, billed him. What I didn't know until years later, when I could more readily understand

Dad's reticence in doing this work, is the owner never paid for the work or services. Mum would always issue a second invoice and then, if not paid, Dad would simply ask her to not send another. It was his way.

I learned the reason why and the inherent lesson when I witnessed a visit by the owner to my parent's business. It was obvious Dad didn't like this man and such disdain poured out of him. The owner asked why Dad wouldn't look at him and Dad simply said, "you don't pay your bills and I am not the only one who knows it. I do the work you need, and I do it only because many in this town need their job at your mill. Without it, they and their loved ones suffer. You are cheap. I do the work and I only do it for them, not you. It's that simple." The man turned on his heels and left. It was later that week when a check arrived for all previous work done. The courier gave the envelope to my dad and he thanked the young man and didn't even open the envelope. He gave it to Mum and asked her to deposit it and then figure out where to donate the funds. He said he didn't want "that" money and he certainly didn't want it from "him." As the years went by, Dad continued to do work for this man and his mill.

Mum would invoice and the bill would be paid. However, any and all payments received were never funds used by our family. They were only to be donated.

Dad's engineering and related work often involved unusual projects and as years passed, he was able to choose projects. He was interested in plastic molding and set out to build the necessary molding and equipment to sport such a venture. He was interested in the burgeoning field of plastics and materials sciences and firms around the country would seek him out, not only for his skill in building customized items but they asked for his advice, as a consultant. This was new for him although a little pride would shine through the normal humble and stoic demeanor.

As years passed, Dad's reputation grew and as he would note later in life, more interesting problems would come to him. He would be visited by professors from the University of Minnesota, or other engineering firms, based in Minneapolis, and then one day, there were a few men in black who knocked on our door. Dressed as they were, it seemed to me, a young girl, this was important. Dad and Mum invited them in, offered coffee and the day's baked goods and they indicated they were from the National Aeronautics and Space Administration (NASA). They were working on something big they said and wanted to speak to Dad privately.

Mum was clearly annoyed since she was central to the business. Nevertheless, she scooped me up and we went to the back small living area and shut the door. I am sure it was minutes, but it seemed like hours. Dad finally called for us and when we emerged he indicated "they," meaning he and Mum, would be working on something new, for the government, and for the future of the country. That was all he said in front of me although he said this was a private matter and I was not to speak of it to anyone. I didn't; nor did I mention it even to the closest of dear friends for decades.

This was the only time the shop was ever locked. And no one but Mum and Dad were to be behind the closed, locked doors. The work was done, Dad was paid, and that was that. I have to believe he and Mum did work for NASA long thereafter, but to what extent and what work was done, remains a mystery. I only know Dad was excited about the work and any contribution they could make.

XIII

THE FAMILY SPUG CLOSET

Everyone should have one, or so my Mum thought. This was a closet for special items Mum referred to as SPUGs, "Some Pretty Ugly Gifts." You know, an item that is gifted to you but, well, isn't all that useful, or beautiful, or whatever. Mum always honored the individual who gave the SPUG since she felt it was heartfelt but honestly, they needed their own special place in our home, the SPUG closet.

She wouldn't dispose of them but rather would resurrect them from the closet when the giver would visit for a meal, coffee, or whatever. I can hear her still today saying, "darling Leslie, would you please go to the SPUG closet and get that pink thing." I'd trot off and collect the item I felt matched the cryptic description and would bring it to her. I would often have a puzzled look on my face and would ask why the item was in the "closet." She smiled, gave me a hug, and told me. She was clear to state she appreciated their intention but also felt it wasn't something she wanted showcased in her home. That was all. She would lovingly wash the item and place it prominently in the living or dining room, depending on the intended purpose of the item. Once the guest or guests were gone, she would again ask me to bring the item to her and she would again give it a bath and ask me to place it back in the SPUG close for safekeeping. This went on for years.

The lesson learned became obvious to me and we would discuss the SPUG closet often. I knew what she meant in creating this space and I always hoped a gift given by me wouldn't end up in someone else's "closet." The lesson was reinforced over and over again in my youth. To be thoughtful and remind oneself of a simple question, "is this something I would value, use, appreciate, or simply enjoy?" If the answer was yes, then you would be safe in the knowledge that the selection was appropriate. If not, to simply wait and tell the person you have something in mind for them, but you haven't quite found it yet. Over the years, I have tried to follow this philosophy and I have often said I am still searching for what I feel they would truly value, appreciate, and enjoy. It's worked, so far.

XIV

WANING DAYS AND PASSAGES

Dad, our father, was first to go. Bernhard Lennart Sandberg died May 24, 1980. The doctors could only suggest the cause of his death was congestive heart failure, and underlying complications associated with Dengue fever. Little did we know he had been slowly dying for nearly six months.

Something was off, and Dad was unusually tired and seemed, at times, to gasp for air. He ignored it believing it was due to long hours and getting older. Mum did, too. It was so unlike her. Her long life in medicine and nursing always made her acutely aware of small changes in people's behavior and she seemed to know when something was amiss. Not this time. I suppose, as is often the case, those closest to us don't want to sense something could be wrong. She was guilty of this and finally acknowledged it following his death. It took a long time for her to come to this conclusion.

As more months passed, it was clear he wasn't improving and our local doctors had no idea what was going on, other than he was exhausted, and his heart was enlarged. He was weak and weary. He was stubborn and ultimately that would prove to help him fight against biology winning, and death too. Mother finally demanded he be moved to Mayo Clinic. Since Mum wanted faster action, we literally drove him to the Mayo Clinic in Rochester, Minnesota. There was silence in the car and while we looked at each other, we all knew what each of us were thinking. We feared the worst but also hoped for a miracle. Any miracle. It didn't come. In the end it would not have mattered to have him there earlier. The dice had been tossed and he had but only days to live. Death was to come for him and he could no longer tough it out. Any quality of life would be nominal, and he knew it. Mum did too.

The experts at Mayo offered more clarity about how he died. They said it was certainly congestive heart failure but there was evidence of Dengue fever. The doctors asked if Dad had spent time in Africa or Asia. Mum only replied that to her knowledge he was stationed in Hawaii but flew throughout the South Pacific. She indicated she had no knowledge of other stopovers during any of his service and flight missions. Mum could only recall one time when he became extremely ill suffering a high fever and body pain. Despite her pleas to see a doctor, Dad only wanted to rest and work when he could. She couldn't convince him. I don't know if my mother knew the true origin of his distress, only that he was very ill and in pain.

The doctors were quiet for what seemed like a long time and then finally one said, "We're shocked he lasted this long. The last six months or so must have been difficult and that he survived as long as he did is a testimony to his innate strength and fortitude." Questions lingered in the air and they asked if they could perform an autopsy. Mum didn't hesitate and simply said, "Yes, it is important to understand more and if it can help others, by all means."

The ride home was quiet. Too quiet. No radio, no discussion, and we all just looked outside the car windows knowing we were in shock and grief. We would never really know all the answers, nor would we relieve ourselves of not seeing any signs or noticing changes we foolishly believed could have made a difference. The questions lingered. Had Dad gotten Dengue during the war? If so, was he infected again and when? Did an original infection of Dengue remain hidden in his body waiting for a biological vulnerability? What was the trigger? Had there been a larger and more widespread Dengue risk throughout the US we didn't know about? Why?

I continued to seek answers for years and read everything I could find. I later worked with a team of researchers and scientists whose research aims to further understand how the Dengue virus causes disease. Much has been learned although Dengue remains a serious health problem worldwide. It remains today the most important mosquito-borne viral disease affecting humans worldwide; tens of millions of cases occur each year resulting in approximately 20,000-25,000 deaths mainly in children. There is currently no vaccine.

Father's death didn't seem to surprise mother as I learned later. She somehow had different memories about his experience with Dengue during WWII. I never asked why she now seemed to remember all this so differently. Perhaps she was in shock knowing he left before her, and just as they were within a week of retiring. They had always put off and delayed so many trips and other adventures and now, as they approached this important week, they were excited about all the new days ahead.

He died as he lived, a quiet, elegant, stoic and serious man. Gentle and kind, forever humble,

I believe he accepted his last days on this earth as he lived. He was too young, only sixty and one month.

When I think of my dad it is usually when I am watching a film or reading something scientific. A feeling comes over me and there he is, in my mind. It happens when I instinctively know he would enjoy what I am watching. A smile comes to me now more than tears and that is a blessing. And then of course, as I listen to music of all kinds, I am reminded of an old and wonderful song by Dan Fogelberg, called "Leader of the Band." It's always been a perfect metaphor in describing my father. You, the reader, may be interested in looking up the lyrics.

Mother went on to live another nine years and most of those years we lived together. We shared a home and learned to live beyond a mother and daughter relationship; be more than mother and daughter. We worked at it. We were of different generations trying to live as roommates, pretending at times not be mother and daughter. It was wonderful and it was difficult. You see, the mother/daughter relationship is always there. Big surprise, eh? I remember asking Mum to call me Leslie and I would call her Shirley. This would, I had hoped, signal a need for a woman-to-woman discussion that was needed or desired. Well, it lasted about one day. The first time I tested the hypothesis and asked "Shirley" to comment on a work situation that distressed me, she happily agreed and grinned. She listened ever so carefully to what I had to say and then went on to offer what she would do if she were in my situation.

I thanked her and said I was going to change clothes so we could grab a bite to eat somewhere. I felt we had arrived at a new relationship level and felt proud we were both able and willing to do this. Of course, that didn't last long. I barely left the dining table when she blurted, "if you want to know what your mother thinks, let her know."

And well, there I was, knowing full well this was a terrible idea. I didn't say anything but simply chuckled to myself. We never spoke that way to each other again. Mum was Mum. And I was her daughter. And there was no changing that or pretending to be anything else.

She would often join me at work, in various meetings and conferences. A fun escape, she seemed to enjoy herself, sitting in a local hotel coffee shop, visiting with others, and of course, reading and drinking endless cups of coffee. I'd worry about her being alone and would check in on her when I could escape from the work of the day. She'd be annoyed and tell me she was fine.

Period. When I hosted a work meeting or project planning event, she would jump into gear and bake well into the wee hours of the morning. We'd pack up the goodies and off we'd go. It didn't take long before I always had 100% attendance. I am confident the meeting and subject at hand wasn't all that riveting but clearly work was done, thanks to her presence and the smell and taste of homemade baked goods. This became part of our natural routine.

Occasionally in these meetings, she would join in and offer her advice and counsel. I suppose one could call it professional parenting. I'd see her raising her hand, as she sat in the back of the room, and I would call on her. I would introduce her to everyone to ensure they knew who she was and that she was my Mum. She'd say hello, remind everyone to eat more, and then tell us to make up our "damned" minds and move forward with the work. Folks would chuckle and find it amusing (I think) but nonetheless, we continued in our efforts and all was well. I regret not telling her how much this meant to me. I hope she knew this but I should have said it far more often.

Shirley Jane Bell Slocumb Sandberg died in her sleep in the wee hours of October 20, 1989. We had planned to spend the following day together, as we often would on weekends; breakfast or brunch, then shopping, and, of course, a good movie. That day wasn't meant to be, and so many other days, too. She hadn't been ill. In fact, a full physical weeks before indicated she was well and strong. I called her doctor the day she died, and he was stunned to know Mum had died. There was a long silence during the phone call, as if we lost the connection, and then he simply said, "shit." He was shocked and angry and asked if he could call the coroner to learn more. I said yes, of course. What he learned and later told me is her heart simply stopped. He was aware she had rheumatic fever as a young woman but to what degree this may have contributed to her death, wasn't validated.

Consequently, since Mum died without any symptoms, the most common reason and one used in my mother's case was "cardiac arrhythmia," specifically ventricular fibrillation or pulseless ventricular tachycardia. My mother would have wanted it this way, and she would have declared this to be simply "a great way to go."

I still feel my parents were cheated out of many good years. It took many years for me to fully accept their passing and fortunately time eventually became a friend. It allows us to know loss is inevitable and any loss, even those that are the most difficult, come to rest more easily in our hearts. I also know there was no fixing them. It doesn't work that way. Biology you see, always overcomes human strength and stubbornness. And even if one clings tenaciously to life, as my parents did, enjoying each moment, in the end, they too had to let go. Death doesn't take a holiday. Fortunately, the love I have for them, and anyone I have lost since, transcends death's grasp.

My parents are both interred at the National Memorial Cemetery of the Pacific (informally known as the Punchbowl Cemetery). It had always been my father's wish to be buried there and mother, too. This national cemetery is located at the Punchbowl Crater in Honolulu, Hawaii. It serves as a memorial to honor those men and women who served in the United States Armed Forces, many who gave the ultimate sacrifice, their lives in doing so. This hallowed resting place is now home for more than 53,000 veterans of three American Wars: WWII, Korean War and the Vietnam War. It is truly the "Cemetery of Heroes." The Punchbowl itself was formed some 75,000 to 100,000 years ago during the secondary volcanic period of Honolulu's history. A crater resulted from the ejection of hot lava through cracks in old coral reefs and extended well to the Koolau Mountain Range. So literally, it is a "bowl."

My father loved the poem High Flight by John Gillespie Magee, Jr. He would recite it often. He would always honor Mr. Magee each time in reminding us all that Mr. Magee was an Anglo-American fighter pilot officer and poet and served with the Royal Canadian Air Force. Born in Shanghai, China, a son of missionary parents, he was an American and his mother was originally a British citizen. He died in a mid-air collision shortly after writing this poem. I suspect my Dad would remember his crew mates, and countless others who didn't make it back home: His face would grow sad when he would recite it but he would smile a bit when finished knowing he had honored the poet and his mates.

High Flight
By John Gillespie Magee, Jr.

Oh! I have slipped the surly bonds of Earth
And danced the skies on laughter-silvered wings.
Sunward I've climbed, and joined the
tumbling mirth
Of sun-split clouds — and done a hundred things
You have not dreamed of — wheeled and
soared and swung.
High in the sunlit silence, hov'ring there
I've chased the shouting winds along and flung
My eager craft through footless halls of air.
Up, up the long delirious burning blue

I've topped the wind-swept heights
with easy grace
Where never lark nor ever eagle flew
And, while with silent, lifting mind I've trod
The high untresspassed sanctity of space,
Put out my hand and touched the face of God.

I've continued over the years to visit their gravesite, walk the grounds of the Punchbowl and always seem to reflect on the many souls buried there. I tour the Arizona Memorial and other historical sites and breathe in the natural beauty of the islands. These visits are always a respite for me since I am again reminded they are at peace. I imagine them whole again, and enjoying the cosmos, meeting historical heroes or doing whatever one does in the next life. That is, if there is one.

XV

UNFULFILLED DREAMS

Everyone can be haunted more by regrets and unfulfilled dreams than by not fulfilling what they believe to be their destiny. Yes, we all have duties and responsibilities, but we owe it to ourselves at some point in our lives to seek that which will bring us the kind of happiness, contentment, and joy we often don't have. My parents were no exception. I always knew Mum had aspirations to follow in her father's footsteps and become a doctor. After all, she worked side by side with her parents in her youth, helping in the clinic and learning all she could about medicine and nursing. This education as I have mentioned was put to good use once the United States entered into WWII and it seems to me now her service would have further fueled her desires. I will not speculate why she was unable or perhaps unwilling to return to her dream of earning a medical degree and when she finally arrived at this decision, or needed to, it didn't seem to trouble her throughout the rest of her life. She didn't allow it to fester or become a source of anger or constant emotional pain. Nor was she bound by her pragmatism in continuing to focus her efforts in helping others in the community. She simply continued to work alongside Dad, help others in the community, often in the role of nurse, or find new ways to lend a hand. In the end, she seemed to discover equal meaning and benefit in doing so.

I have to believe Dad also wanted to further his formal education in engineering but again, such discussion was rare. It was obvious he felt at ease throughout his life in his work and remained immersed in the pursuit of knowledge, a self-educated man of sorts. Such efforts complimented his personality — he could take on a task of gaining knowledge and insight for the sake of one's own benefit. That could be in the form of reading texts, or engineering periodicals, or in testing new ways to accomplish the work at hand. There was no formal curriculum but he always seemed to know what direction to go. Like life, self-education wasn't a linear experience for him. He would act on newfound knowledge, test various theories, and as he often would tell me, "play with it a bit."

One thing I know for certain, each would have continued to pursue their interests in retirement had they been gifted with more time. I can imagine Dad returning to school, and his engineering studies. He wasn't ever able to complete his degree and I know this troubled him. It didn't matter that he was enormously respected by so many professional engineers and professors. He still wanted the degree and the letters after his name. Mum would have continued her deep dive into reading and would have rediscovered languages or new causes to support.

You might be wondering if my parents' unfulfilled dreams or other aspirations were somehow forced upon me. Well no, not really. Did they want me to secure a formal education and become a woman of independent means? Definitely. Did they want me to seek out the best of myself and find meaningful work? Of course. Did they want me to find passion in my life and also be mindful of the realities of the world? Yes. What they did for me, overall, was to open up a world of possibilities to me.

As early as I can remember, they somehow were intent on seeing me as a separate individual, my own person. I never felt I needed to become them or follow in their footsteps. Rather, I would always be fueled by their interest and devotion to what I was thinking about doing or how I wanted to contribute to this world. This has been a comforting thought all these years, to know I was loved exactly as I was, faults and all, and to become the kind of person I am today.

XVI

THE CONSEQUENCES OF LOSS

Not long after Father's death, grief settled in. Grief is about us, the bereaved. I was unable to feel peace about his passing and since I would not be content in losing him for a long time, no matter the circumstances surrounding his death, I just held onto my anger. It wasn't just. Intellectually I knew my grief would be a process and I would eventually take the time needed to work through it, but I wasn't convinced it would ever settle well in my mind. The early stages of grief are always unkind. It is only natural to isolate from others and turn inward. Consequently we become vulnerable. I know I was. I also knew I couldn't remain in that terrible space for long since Mum needed my full attention. Her grief, I felt, was far more catastrophic because her hopes for easier days were stolen. It was obvious that whatever joy she had hoped for was gone and life would be worse without Dad.

After a time, grief turned to stoicism. I suppose we both felt we should no longer punish ourselves further with such sadness. I don't remember when this feeling of trying to move on happened, but it did. I felt it. So did Mum. We somehow were able to speak of Dad's passing in new ways. We reflected on a life well lived. Laughed and cried. And agreed that the people we love or will love will die, and the people we need will die. We will too. More time passed and suddenly we seemed to look at life differently and found new ways to conquer the grief, and there were more good days. Frankly, Dad would have wanted this. He would have wanted us to care deeply about his passing but also be strong enough to soften the reaction to his death. Oddly, these feelings seemed perfectly compatible.

However, I had changed. Somehow I felt my life wouldn't be so very long and whatever years I was granted, they needed to count. I was obsessed with working harder and pushing ahead. I spent less time on fun stuff and more time in pursuing a career and ensuring I could eventually find the time to travel, relax, and so on, but only if I had accomplished as much as possible in the shortest time I could. It is one thing to return to a kind of normal following such a profound loss and function. My forced journey was more of an obsession, or at least that is what Mum called it.

I was encouraged by friends to read the usual grief theorists including Ross, Bowlby, and Parkes and Weiss. I know they were trying to help me soften my pace, but what they didn't know is I had already done all of that. It is in my nature to study things, especially if I can hope to seek a kind of peace and acceptance. None of them slowed my pace and for a long time I worked. Period.

The response I had to my father's passing (and my mother's some years later) in its totality — including its physical, emotional, cognitive and spiritual feelings — was completely natural and normal in my view. Life was going to be different now without him, and we all would be different too. It took a long time to adjust to a life without him.

This is when time again becomes a friend and the bond between my late father and me would continue and remain steadfast even today. I believe spiritually he still protects me and watches over me. He did so when I was a child and often I will think of him and sense his presence. I miss him not calling my name. Then again, it was rare that he would call out my name, Leslie. We all have nicknames and Dad created a few for me. Typical in his quiet loving way, I would hear "Doodle," or "Little One," or "Little Snooks," or "Finker Doo." I never asked how he arrived at these nicknames for me. I regret not doing so. I just always smiled each time he would call out my 'nickname' and go to him. I think of him often. I speak of both my parents and share stories with friends and colleagues. It just seems to pour out of me and feels as natural as breathing.

As a result, I now know I never really let go of either of them. Rather, I never really let them go. It never seemed a requirement. I was eventually successful in my grieving and recognized while they are no longer here, and death ended their lives, it did not end our relationship.

AFTERWORD

Although this homage to my parents has taken literally decades to pen (or perhaps longer in my mind), I now only wish my late parents were here to enjoy reading it. I have tried my best to piece together their stories from my memories and relook at history of times long gone. Of course, finding the occasional photograph helps to freeze such moments linking them to each other. In exploring my memories, not much has changed regarding the perception I hold of my parents although it has brought forward the impact of their passing. I know nobody has perfect parents. I didn't. But I and we learn valuable life lessons from them.

I hope they would be flattered and welcoming of my thoughts and memories. I am certain they would critique and offer their own insights and revisions to content or suggest other improvements. And knowing my mum, she would be sure to tell me where I fell short, or what things or people I neglected to mention. From the first word of this book, I selected and decided (importantly) what to include and what to leave out. I practiced purposeful omission. Writing requires such selection. Regardless, I feel she would be proud I took the time to record my thoughts and would be pleased I have such strong, respectful, and loving memories of her and Father.

They weren't destined to grow old together. There would be no "happily ever after." That was ok. For whatever time they had together, be it short or long, I know they loved a lifetime. This is perhaps the final lesson they taught me. That we can be given a gift of loving someone, and even if the time allotted seems small, one can love and care deeply for another person. And that we should not have regrets in doing so for each minute is precious. After all, we are really only given the day. Mum and Dad always did this, and as such, they gave me hope I could always try to brighten even the darkest moments.

What they taught me in life, they taught me in death: To believe in myself, and in the goodness of people, and to never lose perspective and faith in tomorrow. And finally, to know there are no limits — that I should get up each day, count the day as a blessing and make it the best, and most of all, try always to be kind, forgiving, and humble. I know I have often failed at this over many decades but work daily to live up to their standards and be present in all things. More importantly, I know to go on regardless of circumstances and especially when dark moments are present. They created ways to teach me of the joy in being charitable, and in appreciating kindness, generosity, and friendship. But mostly, I am thankful to them for showing me what pure, unconditional love looks like.

I still find myself wondering what they would have thought about the currency of our days. I am certain much would be shared. I also know they would be saddened by the climate of partisan fury and say calmly it isn't new. Dad would be equally troubled by the lack of protection of the environment and would no doubt lose himself in reading everything he could find on climate change. Mum would be troubled too by this issue although she would focus her disdain and anger on the politics of the day. They both would speak about other moments in our country's history when similar issues became difficult struggles. I know she would tell me to remain hopeful and hold onto such hope. Dad would tell me there would be progress even in the gloomiest moments. His calm stoicism would be reassuring. I would welcome their comments and would enjoy more discussions around the dinner table.

I suppose it is natural we label certain periods in our lives. As I have tried to recount so many memories of my parents, labeling didn't seem to make sense. It wasn't going to give me a stronger image of a specific time in my life with my parents nor did I want to close any of those moments in order to move on. In short, I have become even more comfortable with these memories and they still make me happy.

However one's life may wind down, a lot of emotions come into play. So even if one needs to move on because that is what is supposedly expected of us, I believe it is better to hold onto those emotions in a way that offers excitement about what might be next for each of us. That is what I work on. I am excited to find out what the next chapters of my life will be. I hope to have a long life and am blessed to be where I am in my life at this time. I count each day for what it is, a remarkable blessing. And as Mum would often tell me, "whatever is done is gone; it is time to live again."

A life you see, yours and mine, if well lived, is long enough.

FAVORITE SAYINGS REMEMBERED

I believe we forget so much of what we say, rather than what we hear. And since our bodies have five distinct senses: touch, smell, taste, sight, and hearing, the combinations of these seem to yield so much for us to be experienced. I am free to say this since I so often quote my parents and have included their favorite sayings or quotes in this book. I don't think they realized these would be tattooed onto my memory but it happened.

"Mark my words." (Mum said this infrequently but when said, we all knew to listen carefully. For example, when the first of many articles appeared in the news about the Watergate break in of the Democratic National Headquarters, she announced this loudly indicating she believed this would be the eventual downfall of then President Richard Nixon).

"Manage by the littles."

"It took forever to reach 30 and then I woke up and I was 65."

"You can't beat a man at his own trade."

"Get up! You can sleep when you're dead." (Mum was an early riser and so, I was too. It's not that I don't enjoy quiet slumbers, no matter the time of day, it's just that she would remind me to embrace every hour, since they are precious gifts).

"I would rather have a thimble full of knowledge than a bucket full of B.S." (Dad said this only once. We were driving from Litchfield to Mayo Clinic, Rochester, Minnesota when he said this, hoping they could diagnose him properly and hopefully treat him. This was one week before he died).

"Shit and two makes eight." (Dad said this infrequently and it was stated whenever he made a mistake in his work. I guess the mistake was to be remembered and learned from. What it means, I don't know to this day. He never explained it and sadly, I didn't ask).

"When you awaken each morning commit to making it the best day possible."

"Do things intentionally and not for reason alone."

"Cure first, care later."

"What do you have to complain about?" (Mum would declare this reminding me of the inherent blessings in my life. Even if I felt there was something to complain about, it didn't last long).

"Freewill matters."

"Small steps count."

"Go look it up like I would have to."

"It's only [insert the day]." (Mum would say this frequently reminding me that whatever day it was, there would be another. Basically, not to fret and another day would potentially be better).

"All things are made or created with butter and love."

"If there's no blood on the floor, most everything can be fixed."

"Always hope for happy endings."

"It's a privilege to struggle."

"We'll put num-nums on it to make it better."

"Love deeply."

PHOTOS

The following photos are from an old and sparsely preserved collection and more recently, from visits to my home state, Minnesota, and hometown, Litchfield, Minnesota. Others are from exhaustive research into old archives and of course, some luck using Ancestry.com and Google. I have selected each of these in the hope they will shed light into the lives of my parents and our home in Minnesota. And perhaps add context and background to what I have written on these pages.

There were many other photos I would have loved to include but sadly, as I mentioned earlier, they were all destroyed during the 1991 Berkeley-Oakland firestorm when I lost my home and most family treasures. Since it really wasn't the digital age, those images and the memories and stories they reveal reside now only in my memory.

My mum, Shirley Jane Bell Slocumb Sandberg. This
is also the cover photo for the book. The photo was taken
~1954, a year before I was born.

Photo of Anna Katherine Hess, my great-great grandmother
on my mum's side of the family. A strong and very
independent woman, she was unusual for her time. Source:
Ancestry.com

Spring has arrived and snow is melting. Newer owners of my home in Litchfield, Minnesota, enclosed the porch. Oh the hours I would spend relaxing there with a good book.

Homestead, Litchfield, Minnesota, and the front porch. The holiday lights are still peeking through since winters can be harsh. Too harsh for outdoor activities. I'd often sit on a comfortable lounge chair in the summer reading.

Homestead, Litchfield, Minnesota.
A typical winter growing up.

A view of hometown main street, Litchfield, Minnesota, and
the frequented Hollywood theatre.

The road around Lake Ripley, Litchfield, Minnesota.
If it's winter, there are icy roads.

Classic highway signs close to our small town of Litchfield,
Minnesota. There was one that detailed "Waverly" since it
was the hometown of Hubert Humphrey, 38th Vice
President of the United States. He also served to represent
the State of Minnesota as a U.S. Senator for two terms.

A typical barn near my hometown of
Litchfield, Minnesota. It's rural Minnesota
so agriculture is everywhere.

The amber lobby of the acclaimed Guthrie Theatre,
Minneapolis, Minnesota. It was transformed into a
communal gathering place and now called the Amber
Sanctuary to honor the memory of victims in past shootings
at Sandy Hook Elementary School, Sandy Hook,
Connecticut; at Emanuel African Methodist Episcopal
Church, Charleston, South Carolina; and at Pulse Nightclub,
Orlando, Florida.

Front entrance to the Guthrie Theatre. Designed by Pritzker Prize-winning architect Jean Novel, who shared his vision to reflect the history of the neighborhood. It houses three state-of-the-art stages, production facilities, classrooms, restaurant, and dramatic public spaces.

Called the endless bridge at the Guthrie Theatre, Minneapolis, Minnesota. It is neither endless nor is it a bridge. It offers the single best view of the Mississippi River anywhere along its 2,552 miles length.

One of 23 bridges in Minneapolis and Saint Paul,
Minnesota, that allow pedestrians to walk or drive across
the Mississippi River.

The bird sculpture is a beautiful example of community art, showcased throughout Minneapolis, Minnesota. The bridge above the road is part of the Minneapolis Skyway System. It interlinks a number of enclosed pedestrian footbridges connecting various buildings in 80 full city blocks over 9.5 miles (15.3 km) of downtown Minneapolis, enabling people to walk in climate-controlled comfort year-round. It is the longest continuous system in the world.

The Foshay Tower is a skyscraper in Minneapolis,
Minnesota. Built in 1929 just months before the stock
market crash, it is a superb example of Art Deco
architecture and modeled after the Washington Monument.
When it was built, the thirty-two-story tower was the tallest
building between Chicago, Illinois, and the West Coast. My
father took me
there often to tour the structure.

An old photo of my father's WWII Registration Card. He
was 21. Source: Ancestry.com

The grave marker of my parents remains, interred
at the National Cemetery of the Pacific
(Punchbowl), Honolulu, Hawaii. It was their
wish to be buried together.

APPENDIX

B-24 Liberator units of the United States Army Air Forces. (2019, July 13). In *Wikipedia*. Retrieved from https://en.wikipedia.org/wiki/B-24_Liberator_units_of_the_United_States_Army_Air_Forces

Bernstein, Carl, & Bob Woodward. (1974). *All the President's Men*. Simon and Shuster.

Brokaw, Tom. *The Greatest Generation*. (2000). Random House; 1st Edition.

Buscaglia, Leo. (1972). *Love, A Warm And Wonderful Book About The Largest Experience In Life*. Fawcett Crest Books.

Caldecott Tunnel Fire. (1991). In *Wikipedia*. Retrieved from https://en.wikipedia.org/wiki/Caldecott_Tunnel_fire

Camp Atterbury. (2020, September 6). In *Wikipedia*. Retrieved from https://en.wikipedia.org/wiki/Camp_Atterbury

Consolidated B-24 Liberator. (2020, July 8). In *Wikipedia*. Retrieved from https://en.wikipedia.org/wiki/Consolidated_B-24_Liberator

Dickinson, Emily, & Thomas H. Johnson. (2012). *The Poems of Emily Dickinson*. Start Publishing LLC.

Fogelberg, Dan. *Leader of The Band*. The Innocent Age (1981). Sony/ATV Music Publishing LLC. Retrieved from https://www.lyrics.com/lyric/814582/Dan+Fogelberg/Leader+of+the+Band

Giant. (2012, June 28). In Indiana Military Org. Retrieved from http://www.indianamilitary.org/WakemanHospital/Departments/BlockerCol.htm

Gibbons, Robert V et al. "Dengue and US military operations from the Spanish-American War through today." *Emerging infectious diseases* vol. 18,4 (2012): 623-30. doi:10.3201/eid1804.110134

Google Scholar: Fuller, J.F. (1990) World War II Pacific. In: Thor's Legions. American Meteorological Society, Boston, MA. https://doi.org/10.1007/978-1-935704-14-0_7

Hailey, Elizabeth Forsythe. (1998). *A Woman of Independent Means*. Penguin Books.

High Flight. (1999, May 22). In Arlington Cemetery. net. Retrieved from http://www.arlingtoncemetery.net/highflig.htm

History of the US Army Air Corps in Hawaii Dept. (2020). In Aviation.Hawaii.gov. Retrieved from https://aviation.hawaii.gov/airfields-airports/oahu/hickam-fieldair-force-base/history-of-the-us-army-air-corps-in-hawaii-dept-2/

It's Our War, Too! The WAC at Camp Atterbury During WWII. (2015, March 23). Indiana State Library, blog. library.IN.GOV. Retrieved from https://blog.library. in.gov/tag/camp-atterbury-world-war-ii/

Keillor, Garrison, & Marcia Pankake. (1999). *A Prairie Home Companion Commonplace Book: 25 Years on the Air with Garrison Keillor*. Highbridge Company.

Minnesota Digital Library. Retrieved from https:// mndigital.org

Minnesota Historical Society. Retrieved from https:// www.mnhs.org/

Minnesota Reflections. Retrieved from https:// reflections.mndigital.org

Monahan, Evelyn, & Rosemary Neidel-Greenlee. (2007). *And If I Perish: Frontline U.S. Army Nurses in World War II*. Anchor.

National Memorial Cemetery of the Pacific. (2020, September 1.) In *Wikipedia*. Retrieved from https://

en.wikipedia.org/wiki/National_Memorial_
Cemetery_of_the_Pacific

Norris, Kathleen. (1996). *The Cloister Walk*. Riverhead
Books.

Oakland Firestorm of 1991. (2020, September 10). In
Wikipedia. Retrieved from https://en.wikipedia.org/
wiki/Oakland_firestorm_of_1991

Pietrusza, David. (2018). 1948: *Harry Truman's
Improbable Victory and the Year that Transformed
America*. Diversion Books.

Punchbowl Crater. (2020, April 9). In *Wikipedia*.
Retrieved from https://en.wikipedia.org/wiki/
Punchbowl_Crater

Remembering Maya Angelou. (2020). In *Writers &
Books, bring words and people together*. Retrieved
from https://wab.org/remembering-maya-angelou/

Snow, G. E., Haaland, B., Ooi, E. E., & Gubler, D. J.
(2014). Review article: Research on dengue during
World War II revisited. *The American journal of
tropical medicine and hygiene, 91*(6), 1203–1217.
https://doi.org/10.4269/ajtmh.14-0132

The Army Nurse Corps. (2020). WW2 US Medical
Research Centre. Retrieved from https://www.med-
dept.com/articles/the-army-nurse-corps/

"The Secret of Don Hewitt's Success." 60 Minutes, presented by Steve Kroft. CBS. August 21, 2009.

Watergate Scandal. (2019, September 25). In *History. com.* Retrieved from https://www.history.com/ topics/1970s/watergate

ABOUT THE AUTHOR

Leslie Sandberg graduated from the University of Arkansas, where she earned a bachelor's degree in Gerontology and Urban Affairs. She also holds a Master's in Business Administration from Saint Mary's College. She has held key roles in the private and public sector and served on numerous advisory boards focused on health care policy and technology development. She served on several state and national committees focused on healthy aging initiatives. She was a senior fellow with the Center for the New West, Denver, Colorado, and served as the Executive Director of their Institute for Telemedicine. During her career she chaired the Healthcare Working Group of the National Information Infrastructure Testbed (NIIT).

A native Minnesotan, she now calls California home and enjoys travel, theatre, and spending time with her closest friends. https://www.linkedin.com/in/leslieasandberg

9 781839 753794